THOSI Conjecture

(Second Edition)

- THOSI is the initials of the five most important factors or geographical plus climatic conditions that affect the evolution of human DNA as carried by the generations living somewhere in a continent or island, i.e. temperature, humidity, oxygen concentration, sunlight intensity and isolation extent, which are explained further below.

- Temperature: it is widely viewed that somewhere around 20 degrees Celsius / 68 degrees Fahrenheit is the temperature in which human beings (no matter what ethnic groups we are talking about) feel most comfortable (hereinafter referred to as the Golden Temperature or GT). The closer to GT, the more comfortable, the better human organs function and ultimately the better for human beings evolution.

- Humidity: speaking of livability, people usually care more about temperature than humidity without realizing that humidity is actually an equally important factor affecting our living environment. It is widely viewed somewhere between 40% and 50% is the best humidity for human beings with healthy or normal respiratory system.

- Oxygen concentration or density: the term shall refer to the quantity of oxygen per liter and as a result the quantity of oxygen per inhalation, which is of course associated with and affected by other factors like green coverage, altitude, air pressure and temperature etc., but due to its more immediate impact on functioning and evolution of human brains and higher representativeness compared with the aforesaid factors, it would be better to give it a seat in THOSI. The author cannot find the source specifying the best oxygen concentration except that it usually stays around 21% and it will cause damage to health if it falls below 19.5% or 19%, but surely there should be a golden level of oxygen concentration from human comfort and evolution perspectives.

- Sunlight intensity: this mainly refers to ultraviolet rays plus brightness. The closer to the tropics, and/or the higher altitude, the more sunlight intensity. Even in one certain place sunlight intensity may fluctuate with the change of seasons, but based on most people's experiences and feelings, it should be accepted that the best sunlight intensity lies on certain latitude somewhere between the tropics and the poles within certain range of altitude.

- Isolation extent: this refers to the extent that a geographical place in a continent is isolated from the other parts of the said continent by mountains or from other continents by oceans. If the isolation extent of a certain area, where the above said conditions are good for human species, is very high, then the human beings residing in such area can enjoy peaceful and steady evolution, and more importantly, can absorb competitive

DNA immigrating from those remote areas and other continents. The only difference between isolation extent and the above-said four conditions is that isolation extent changes a lot with the increasing convenience of long-distance transportation as a result of science and technology development, while the other factors remain far more steady. For example, the isolation extent of West Europe has declined substantively due to the fact that today it is much more convenient for people in Africa, Middle East and West/Central Asia to travel or even immigrate into West Europe than it was centuries ago.

• Mathematical THOSI-evaluation. Taking temperature as an example, we can sketch a chart (vertical line for temperature and horizontal for time) to lay out the temperatures of the 365 days in a climatically ordinary year and then draw the curve to demonstrate the temperature change on an annual basis. In addition, we can draw a straight horizontal line representing the GT, and then easily calculate the area between GT line and the curve. In conclusion, the smaller the area in between, the more comfortable for human beings and consequently better for human beings evolution, and vice versa. For humidity, oxygen density and sunlight intensity, we may follow this approach for calculating such crosshatched areas accordingly so as to measure them in a precise or mathematical way. For isolation extent, it is difficult to do the calculation because: 1) it is affected by mountains, rivers and oceans as well as border control and immigration policies; and 2) as said above, the development in transportation may cause substantive change to the cost of immigration and hence isolation extent. Nevertheless, we may still set a rough categorization system for the main areas of the world and rank them from 1 to 5, with 1 representing the most isolated extent while 5 referring to the least. For example, Japan, as an island country, is surrounded by deep water and at the same time adopts a very strict visa system plus immigration policy, and hence its isolation extent should be ranked at level 1. And the same goes to the UK, Iceland, Australia and New

Zealand.

- THOSI Scores. Here are a few issues to be considered for calculating THOSI scores. First, for those countries with huge area like Russia, Canada, Brazil, Australia, China and USA, it is infeasible to comprehensively evaluate such climatic conditions as temperature and humidity etc. because they vary quite a lot from north to south as well as from east to west. Thus the THOSI conditions in these countries should be measured separately, i.e. breaking them down to at least five parts, including northwest, northeast, southeast, southwest plus the central and calculating THOSI scores for each part of them respectively as the first step, and then calculating their overall THOSI scores (i.e. average scores) as the second step. Second, we may adopt the above-said 1-5 ranking system to the remaining THOSI factors to ensure the consistency, i.e. the smaller area indicating the better result, and corresponding to the lower number of level. Thirdly, it is unclear whether any of these five factors should be more or less weighted when aggregating the final THOSI scores because of their more or less importance in human DNA evolution. There of course should be more scientific input in this regard, which is way beyond the author's and even anthropologist's expertise and capability. Based on the assumption that all five conditions be equally weighted, we can conclude that the most ideal THOSI scores should be five, i.e. $1+1+1+1+1= 5$ while the worst being 25. Notwithstanding the above, the author still holds the view that oxygen concentration is probably the most important factor in terms of human brain evolution. In other words, human beings in those places with the best oxygen concentration level (most probably in those cold and low-altitude areas) may have relatively high average IQ.

• G7 under THOSI Conjecture. From the author's limited personal traveling experiences and knowledge, the following countries and areas may have the best (or lowest) THOSI scores:

USA, Canada, Australia, Europe (strictly speaking excluding those areas near Asia), Japan, New Zealand, and South Korea (hereinafter collectively referred to as the Group of Seven or G7). So under THOSI Conjecture, the high level of economic development and civilization of G7 shall not be attributed to political structure, culture, history, religion or so-called possibilism, but mainly if not purely is the result of geographical determinism (for clarification the term of geographical determinism herein has different meaning from what it meant in the past). In other words, the superior THOSI status of G7 determines the features (intentionally avoiding choosing the word quality for respect of humanity and avoidance of racism but these two terms are interchangeable from academic point of view) of human DNA either living in these areas, and then further shapes the remaining aspects ranging from human appearance, societal average IQ (as the most decisive factor), culture, values, religion and language to civilization, political structure, economy, science and technology etc., i.e. almost everything in human societies.

- Harmonization between THOSI Conjecture and Out-of-Africa Theory. As a widely accepted theory in anthropology, human beings as the most intellectual mammal species on earth originated in Africa. Some of our ancestors walked out of Africa and then entered and settled in other parts of the world. Speaking of the relationship between the THOSI Conjecture and the Out-of-Africa Theory, they should not be contradictory to each other, but co-exist in harmony. There is certainly tons of work to do for explaining why through hundreds of thousands of years of human beings' activities, today different races or ethnic groups are occupying different areas on the planet, but it should be safe to say that as a result of such long-term activities, more competitive human beings have occupied more comfortable places (i.e. with superior THOSI status), while less competitive human beings have occupied less comfortable places (i.e. with inferior THOSI status). Such long-term competition process in its essence should be no different from the fact that though free competition in NY, more competitive DNA occupies Manhattan and the less competitive occupies Brooklyn. For clarification, such analogy is not discriminative against any individual living in Brooklyn in that the term DNA herein is used on an average basis and there are certainly quite a number of individuals in Brooklyn who are above the average competitiveness of Manhattan residents, just like the comparison between Harvard and other universities as discussed below. Furthermore, through competition (of course on the condition that free competition still works in the society which is however another irrelevant issue herein), the current residents in Manhattan and Brooklyn and/or their offspring may respectively experience ups and downs and therefore from time to time some of them may dramatically switch their residences. So this is a process full of changes, dynamics and uncertainty.

- THOSI and human DNA evolution. In those areas with

superior THOSI status, human DNA may evolve in a better direction and with higher velocity than those areas with inferior THOSI status. The most significant result is that the average IQ of human beings in THOSI-superior places becomes higher than in THOSI-inferior places. For a human society, the most decisive factor for its success or failure is exactly the societal average IQ of its members.

• White Caucasians and THOSI Conjecture. Although not every white Caucasian is genetically superior and there are quite many brilliant people in other ethnic groups, it is an undeniable fact that the most important and most shining human achievements in civilization plus science and technology have been primarily based on the innovative contributions mainly made by the people in Mediterranean in particular Greece in ancient time, then Roman Empire in Middle Ages, afterwards West Europe during Industrial Revolution and more recently the USA, all of which are unexceptionally white Caucasians majority societies. So the sharp question is whether white Caucasians as an ethnic group are truly genetically superior to or in other words have higher average IQ than other ethnic groups. This is a quite complicated issue, but seemingly we can still find a clue under the guidance of THOSI Conjecture. The possible process could be like this: the most competitive human beings left Africa long time ago, moved to and then successfully settled in northern or European part of Mediterranean where its THOSI status was comparatively superior to that in Africa and other neighboring areas. The evidences proving higher average societal IQ in such area include: 1) civilization level was the highest in terms of agriculture, science & technology, literature, art, social and political structure, and hygienic conditions (e.g. in ancient Greece, the drainage and sewerage systems were simply unimaginable contemporarily in other parts of the world, not to mention a comparison between them); and 2) according to the results of the wars between ancient Greece and its enemies, people in ancient Greece were militarily superior to other ethnic groups. Thus the possible genetic superiority of Caucasians is not because of their whiteness or skin color. The ultimate truth could be just a simple fact that a bunch of human beings walked out of Africa for whatever reasons, and though long-time competition the smartest ones occupied the THOSI-superior northern or European part of the Mediterranean, and with the increase of population some of them moved further up to the north in Europe and in the past centuries migrated to America, Canada, Australia and New Zealand. Along with the THOSI change, in particular sunlight intensity and temperature, this particular group of human beings evolved into a new ethnic group, i.e. white Caucasians with lighter color of skin, eyes and hair (possibly because of less melanin) as accompanied by other appearance changes. In short, white people are smarter not because they are white, but because certain number of smart or competitive descendants of our African ancestors moved to and occupied the north where they became smarter and more competitive later on, and as a side effect of living in the north for tens of thousands of years, turned white eventually. Another important point herein is that it is only the AVERAGE IQ of white Caucasians is higher than most, if not all, of the other ethnic groups (since Japanese are probably equally smart or even a little bit smarter than white Caucasians, which will be discussed later). In other words, from individual perspective, there are certainly quite many smart people in other ethnic groups whose IQ can reach or even surpass the average IQ of white Caucasians. We can make an analogy here to make this point easier to comprehend, e.g. the average IQ of the students in Harvard University is probably the highest among the universities in the USA or even in the world, which however cannot exclude the likelihood or deny the fact that quite many students in those second-tier or even third-tier universities are of IQ well above the average IQ of Harvard students, some of whom are simply not so lucky to go to Harvard or cannot make it for whatever reasons other than IQ.

- Absorption of competitive DNA through immigration. On one side, G7 are more or less isolated from other parts of the world, but on the other side such isolation may play an important role in absorbing competitive DNA from non-G7 areas, and hence functions a bit like a filter system, i.e. those competitive DNA with better perception, execution ability, and health conditions (i.e. quality DNA) may filter through such system, join the more civilized target society and ultimately make it stronger without breaking the peaceful and steady evolution of the local (i.e. formerly settled) human beings living in such society. The more isolated, the more competitive DNA may filter through. From that perspective, the USA, Canada, Japan, Australia and New Zealand have much better isolation extent than Europe due to their geographical locations. In addition, such absorption process also takes place within G7 because of the THOSI-voltage caused by the THOSI difference between members to G7.

• Non-G7 areas function as quality DNA production/supply pool. As discussed above, from individual perspective, people in those non-G7 areas are unnecessarily less smart than people in G7 although the average societal IQ in such areas may be lower. In addition, due to DNA mutation, the offspring of less smart people may have the chance of carrying high-IQ genes. Therefore, the global trend is that there have always been smart and competitive people making their best efforts to immigrate into G7. So from a macro perspective, the non-G7 areas can be regarded as a giant natural DNA production pool which keeps supplying quality genes to nourish and sustain G7 and hence makes the latter stay unshakably superior. But on the other hand, it is equally noteworthy that in G7 certain low-IQ-related genes are largely reproduced and high-IQ-related genes may also mutate unfortunately for the worse, therefore you can always find that a good portion of native people in G7 are less smart than those merit-oriented immigrants who have achieved success in G7 on the basis of their intelligence and diligence.

According to scientific research, IQ-related genes are intensively allocated on X chromosome and such allocation is highly disproportionate with the total number of the genes on X chromosome. There is also a Chinese saying that a stupid father only results in his own stupidity while a stupid mother ruins all her kids. Furthermore, a lot of people interestingly believe that marrying a smart man may be challenging for a girl because she has to deal with a smart mother-in-law behind her son, which can also be put in a positive way like this, i.e. to marry a smart woman's son is a blessing because he must be smart as well. If the theory that X chromosome carries more IQ-related genes is true, then encouraging or stimulating smart women to give birth to as many babies as they can could be the smartest public policy for a government since what ultimately matters most for a society is its average IQ level, although identifying smart women requires very delicate and sophisticated legislative skills.

- Political structure and societal DNA quality. Hypothetically we can assume there is such a minimum IQ level that enables an individual to fully understand and firmly hold that the success of a society in the modern world is subject to such fundamental elements regarding social structure as democracy, freedom of speech / press / association / assembly / petition, power separation, checks and balances, free and independent media, non-politicalization of the military, limited terms of presidency, etc. In other words, the aforementioned individual is smart enough to understand that monopoly is always worse than free competition either in terms of economy or politics and hence prefers to live in a democratic and liberal system rather than a totalitarian and dictatorial one, and on the other hand, it is quite difficult or costs too much to trade with this person for his democratic rights. For convenience in analysis on this issue, we may define such IQ level as the Minimum Democratic-society IQ or MDIQ. For those who have MDIQ or higher IQ, they can be called A-DNA carrier, and for those with IQ below MDIQ, they can be labelled as B-DNA carrier (just for avoidance of any doubt, B-DNA carriers should have the same fundamental human rights as A-DNA carriers except for the political voting rights as discussed later on). Of course such definition and classification are just for convenience of analysis while the reality in terms of the societal IQ level could be a much more complicated spectrum. The mechanism for selection of political structure may process like this: when the proportion of A-DNA carriers in a society reaches certain percentage (just like in chemistry the temperature of some sort of stuff reaching the ignition point), then such society may automatically or naturally choose democratic political structure instead of totalitarian one in the modern world with the spark of certain incident, while in case of lower percentage, the result may go to the opposite or such system as determined by the outside forces (e.g. colonization in the 19th century, and the current political systems in Iraq and Afghanistan as established with the USA's "help"). Such watershed percentage should be under 50%

simply because A-DNA carriers are politically more influential and more capable than B-DNA carriers. So we may further assume that the said watershed percentage is probably around 40% (which could be somehow associated with the golden ratio (i.e. 1-0.618), and is hereinafter referred to as the Watershed Percentage or WP). But for clarification, the WP does not mean a golden percentage, because the higher societal average IQ, the more successful for the society, but only refers to such a minimum percentage that may trigger the choice of democratic system on the basis of societal self-awareness.

• Consistency between MDIQ and scholarly IQ. Many people think that a person's political views and attitudes are completely or mainly a social construct (i.e. influenced by his or her family, social status, education, life and work experiences, etc.). However, there have been some research and study suggesting that there is somehow a correlation between genes and political views plus attitudes, implicating that there are probably more fundamental or genetic reasons for different people holding different political views and attitudes. To the best of the author's knowledge, those with MDIQ or higher IQ are usually academically more intelligent (i.e. having better performance and higher scores when in school or university) than those who are against the afore-said democracy-oriented values and supportive of totalitarianism-oriented mindset. The opponents may argue that such phenomenon in itself is exactly the result of social influence, or specifically speaking, those academically more intelligent people usually have higher linguistic ability (i.e. English proficiency) and hence can better understand and absorb the western ideology, and therefore are more influenced by such ideology. But such argument seems to confirm rather than deny the conclusion that there is consistency between the defined MDIQ and academic IQ since academic IQ may well represent generalized human IQ. Under the THOSI Conjecture, from IQ perspective, the political structure in a THOSI-superior society would evolve in this process flow: 1) the superior THOSI conditions speed up human DNA evolution and concurrently absorb more competitive DNA from other areas; 2) the average societal IQ keeps climbing; 3) when the percentage of A-DNA carriers reaches certain level or so-called critical point (i.e. WP), the whole society, with the spark of certain incident, may automatically switch to democratic political system though historically speaking such switching process is more time-consuming and complicated; 4) the self-grown democratic political system may fully exploit individuals' potential and ultimately make the society flourish.

- Essential elements of IQ. Though IQ can be tested through different means (ranging from maths, linguistics, spatial intelligence, memory and logics etc.), the essential or materialized elements of IQ should remain the same. A comparison between human brains and smart phones may well demonstrate the essential elements of human IQ. As compared with the parts and components of a smart phone, human IQ can be measured in the following aspects: 1) general thinking power consisting of calculating, analyzing, reasoning plus logical, divergent, innovative, creative and spatial thinking, etc. (as opposed to CPU/GPU-related functions); 2) ability to memorize data and information (as opposed to memory and hard disk for data input, output and storage); 3) coordination and harmonization between different parts of brain (as opposed to main board); and 4) durability or long-time consecutive thinking ability (as opposed to battery life). Among the above-listed four elements, durability is probably the most precious one as there are quite many smart people around us but very few of them can be both smart (referring to the other three elements) and persistently smart (referring to durability). Therefore, durability is objectively a rarer human genetic resource, and hence the market value of such resource is extremely high. That well explains why only a small portion of smart people can be very successful eventually. It's simply because they can be much more intensive and productive in particular when working on multiple projects concurrently. From human resource management perspective, these genetically lucky people can stay on the top or center to coordinate with multiple directions and aspects for a long period of time without losing their thinking power. Such arrangement is certainly more feasible and more efficient than putting multiple smart people in the center to cope with multiple aspects because its coordination cost would be too high to afford. Therefore, the remuneration for these persistently-smart people is not and should not be determined by how many times their durability is longer than others, but exclusively how rare such human DNA resource is in the talent market. So for those smart people without too much durability element, we probably should not blame their laziness or lack of persistence or attitudes for their failure or being not so successful, because they are just genetically not so lucky.

• Environmental influence on IQ. Whether IQ is primarily determined by genes or surrounding environment often arouses debates. The above-said comparison between human brain and smartphone may help explain the issue. First of all, if IQ is a term only associated with human brains as opposed to hardware in smartphones rather than knowledge, experience, cognition and way of thinking etc. as data and information stored in human brains as opposed to software or operation system installed in smartphones, then genes are definitely dominant or decisive. But if IQ refers to both hardware and software in human brains, then such analysis would be quite messy, chaotic and meaningless simply because you cannot tell which iPhone is smarter, i.e. an iPhone X with IOS 7 plus only a few apps or an iPhone 5 with IOS 12 and quite many apps. For individuals, what we care most is their hardware instead of software simply because the former is unchangeable while the latter is not so. But even if IQ only refers to hardware in our brains, environment still has supplementary impact thereon. Such environmental factors mainly include, among others, nutrition, oxygen, external damage, trauma and intellectual training or exercising during human brain growing process. From THOSI perspective, the THOSI conditions, in particular oxygen condition may have very tiny and imperceptible influence on human brain development in a single generation, but the incremental effect on human brain evolution through hundreds of thousands of years may be substantial and more importantly may cause huge societal differences in terms of culture, politics, economy, science and technology etc.

• Layout of societal IQ-related human DNA resources. Let's assume that human IQ can be precisely measured through testing or medical instrument or even DNA analysis in the future, and hence theoretically speaking, we can make a cylindric matrix (with the vertical referring to IQ level) to layout all individuals' IQ scores in a society. The result could be a spectrum-like layout with the following features: 1) the change from top to middle and then to bottom is gradual rather than abrupt; 2) the thickness or density increases from top to middle, and then drops from middle to bottom; 3) the percentage of the very top is close to that of the very bottom, and hence the whole layout vertically seems symmetric; 4) the relatively thick or dense part around the center area (i.e. ordinary IQ level) is the majority while the thin parts at top and bottom (i.e. extraordinarily high / low IQ) being two minorities at two extremes. Such societal IQ layout should basically correlate with the structure of allocation of wealth or other resources in a society, i.e. middle class accounting for the majority while the top rich and homeless or those living in extreme poverty being minorities. The above-said features should unanimously exist for both sides of G7 and non-G7 areas, except that the size of middle-class majority could be different in specific countries, i.e. the center area in the matrix could look more or less thick or dense. In addition, due to the constant flow of quality genes from non-G7 to G-7, the middle part may shrink in certain non-G7 areas but flourish in G7, and the former may decline to be pyramid-shaped societies while the latter solidly remains olive-shaped.

- Societal consensus ratio and societal average IQ level. The higher IQ two persons have, the more easily they can communicate with each other, appreciate one another's correctness in their fundamental opinions, and spot one another's defects, and then the more likely they will eventually reach agreement on specific issues. Even if they are from very different cultural backgrounds and initially hold very different views, their high IQ will help them quickly spot their genuine differences and realize on each side what are the views that do make sense and what are the wrong ideas caused by problematic culture or social environment in particular misleading propaganda. On the contrary, if two persons are unfortunately of extreme low IQ and happen to hold very different views, opinions or values, then it can be well imagined and often experienced in our real life that they can hardly conduct effective communication with each other because it requires certain IQ level to do the same as in the above-described hypothetical case. So what's left for them to do is just sticking to their own sides, repeating what they already know, and being ignorant about what the other side says or holds true. So when some people say that the biggest gap between people is the gap between their different values, they are actually wrong, because ultimately the gap is simply between their different IQ levels. So from this perspective, we can explain why the societal consensus ratio in G7 is obviously higher than that in other areas, and consequently why such society can reach a real constitution that governs the whole society, i.e. rule-of-law society. And this may to certain extent explain why constitutions in G7 can be taken seriously and well implemented while constitutions in most of the other areas, no matter how thoroughly and delicately they are drafted, exist in name only and perform practically no function. Furthermore, it also explains why in civil and commercial activities, contracts in most cases can be better honored and performed in G7 but cannot be taken too seriously in those non-G7 areas. Many people blame culture, history, economic development or other kinds of cliché like those for such difference without knowing the reason is actually very simple, and that is the gap between different THOSI conditions and the consequential different societal average IQ levels as well as the different social structures.

• Success of Japan. Japan is widely viewed as the most developed and most civilized or generally speaking, the best country in Asia. Many people hold the view that such success was due to Meiji Reform, which truly over-simplifies the causes for the vast differences between Japan and other Asian countries. However, under the THOSI Conjecture, the success of Japan can be examined and explained from a completely different perspective. First of all, the following facts can be viewed as the evidence to prove the very difference between Japan and the rest of Asia: 1) the emperor of Japan has never changed, which seems very contrary to the chaotic dynasty-changes in its neighbor China, and such political neatness and tidiness as well as stability may reflect the creditworthiness, good faith, discernment and integrity of Japanese; 2) it only took Japan roughly 20 years to complete its industrialization process and then become one of the most powerful and wealthy countries in the world after Meiji Reform; 3) after WWII, it took about 20 years, again, for Japan as a defeated country in debris, to become the second largest economy, ranked only after the US; 4) Japan was only defeated by the US in WWII, but has never been conquered by any outside force in its history; 5) in Yuan Dynasty (a sovereign state established by Mongolians with its capital in Beijing China), China waged two wars against Japan, aiming to conquer the island, but lost both of them. The military forces mainly consisted of Mongolians, Koreans and Chinese. According to historical records on the Chinese side, typhoons should be blamed for both failures. However, the historical records on the Japanese side show that 1) the approach of using too many war horses was a bad idea; 2) lack of well-trained warriors good at maritime war was another reason; and 3) the sharp and deadly swords used by Japanese warriors played an important role in defeating their enemy. Usually speaking, the testimony of winning side is more convincing. Furthermore, the creditworthiness of Japanese is far beyond the rest of Asia. Thus we may take the Japanese records more seriously. Besides, it should be noted that the sharpness and deadliness of Japanese swords may well represent the average societal IQ of Japanese as metallurgy can be regarded as the highest-technology industry in ancient time. Secondly, the achievements on science and technology made by Japanese in modern time are also shockingly and disproportionately fantastic, which can be reflected by the long list of high-tech pioneering corporations plus Nobel laureates and so many other indicators. Thirdly, the hygienic conditions and social order plus etiquette in Japan are way beyond the rest of Asia and even quite many in G7. Fourthly, Japan is actually very poor in natural resources (except for beautiful scenery) and suffers a lot from earth quakes, but these negative factors have never deterred Japanese from achieving those amazing goals one by one. If we stick to explaining such phenomena only from so-called historical, cultural, educational or political perspective, we are simply cheating or paralyzing ourselves or just lack some courage and sincerity to accept the very truth from geographical or THOSI perspective and on a genetic basis.

• Limited success of Japan in science and technology innovation. Although Japan is a very successful country in Asia and even the whole world, its contribution to science innovation is however limited, especially if compared with Europe and the US. Such limitedness could be attributed to the limited flatland area of Japan, which capped and still caps the population of Japanese. Due to limited population, the capacity for creativity, innovation and originality is also negatively affected as a result of limited number of geniuses, or in other words human beings with super-IQ-related genes.

- China v. Japan. A comparison between China and Japan may show that Japan is obviously THOSI-superior to China in all five aspects. But it should be noted that the population in China is over ten times as much as in Japan. Therefore, under the THOSI Conjecture, although the average IQ of Japanese as well as A-DNA Carrier percentage is higher than in China, the absolute number of A-DNA Carriers in China could possibly be higher than in Japan. This may explain why today we can see so many smart and civilized people in China in particular in those megacities like Shanghai, Beijing, and Shenzhen but it's still far behind Japan in both social and economic aspects in particular living conditions despite its economic aggregate calculated in GDP. In other words, Japan is undoubtedly a country standing way above Watershed Percentage while the percentage of A-DNA Carriers in China is very likely more or less below the WP. Notwithstanding the above, however, even though China adopts a totalitarian system, it's more successful than most of the other

Asia countries some of which are even democratic states, e.g. India and Pakistan. Therefore, what is decisive is not about what kind of political system a country adopts, but is exactly and ultimately the average societal IQ level, which is exclusively based on its THOSI status.

• Impact of political system on success or failure of a country. First of all, this is actually a pseudo-proposition in most cases. Many people hold the view that a good political system may exploit the good merits in people while a bad one may stimulate their badness and thus political system is highly decisive for the success of a sovereign country. And under this theory, they believe too much in so-called good political system and ignore the very fact that good political system can only be created by "enough good people", i.e. sufficient percentage of A-DNA Carriers. There is a very subtle causality mistake herein, i.e. mistakenly regarding the good system as the cause on top while neglecting there is something more decisive beyond the system on the logical tree, i.e. THOSI status and the ensuing human genetic quality, in particular societal IQ level. Therefore, it is of little significance and even dangerous to conduct hypothetical analysis on what a country would be like if it adopts a different political system, because the social system is what naturally grows out of the soil with certain THOSI conditions and the consequent societal average IQ level as well as the percentage of A-DNA Carriers. Objectively there is always compatibility between the people in a country and its self-determined political system at certain historical stage. If this country is forced by any external power to adopt a different political system which is incompatible with its average genetic quality, then what happens next is usually as follows: 1) the country, if small enough, may have a temporary success under the governance by the external power and/or its local agency; 2) the cost of the said governance gets increasingly high due to the inferior THOSI status of the said country plus the incompatibility between such governance and the country's own genetic quality, and it is particularly so in case of those big countries like India and China; 3) the country will get stuck in chaotic and messy situation because of the said incompatibility after the external force evacuated from the country; 4) the natural power as driven by its THOSI status will push the country to go back to the orbit that it belongs to. The specific cases in countries like China, India, Russia, South Africa, Turkey and the countries in the Middle East etc. may look slightly different from the above-described process, but the general principle under THOSI Conjecture remains unchanged. We will discuss some of these countries later on.

• Impact of political system on individual's personal development. As discussed above, a country's political system is supposed to be what grows out of its own DNA soil or genetic environment and hence in most cases it is of little significance to discuss what kind of political system works best for a country's success. Nevertheless, the impact of political system on an individual's success or failure is however a very meaningful topic. Usually speaking, two genetically identical persons (i.e. twins), with one growing up in India or Iran as the place of his birth and the other in the US as his adoptive parents' home country, would end up with very different life achievements, certainly with more likelihood that the US one achieves more and better and enjoys a more successful life. This is partly because the political system and social structure in G7 can exploit, to a larger extent, the potential in individuals due to more transparent, efficient, merit-oriented, positive-feedback-based or generally speaking fairer human DNA competition environment. Therefore, the significance of political system over individual's development is obvious and undeniable. However, this conclusion in itself is not at all contradictory to the afore-discussed one, i.e. a country's self-grown political system is the result of its societal genetic quality in particular so-called societal average IQ level, and is critically subject to its A-DNA carriers percentage or density, and ultimately there is compatibility or balance between such genetic environment and its self-grown or independently chosen political system. Therefore, it is against human evolution science to force a country to adopt a political system that is over-advanced for and thus incompatible with the said country, which usually ends up with chaotic and messy situation. This looks very much similar to the compatibility between a computer's hardware conditions and the operation system software. We all know that Windows 10 is surely much better and more powerful than Windows 97. But it's surely a bad idea if we try to install Windows 10 on an outdated IBM T20. It simply does not work or works very slowly and unstably. Based on the above discussion, we may find and conclude that it is a dangerous way of reasoning to think that since a certain kind of more advanced political system works better for an individual, it is therefore good for the whole country to abandon its existing system and embrace the said more advanced one. Such reasoning is simply logically wrong though the purpose or motivation is good.

- Impact of natural resources on societal success. It is widely held that abundance in natural resources, especially energy-related and industrialization-needed ones, is a pivotal factor for societal success. However, generally speaking, it is basically a neutral factor in terms of its influence over societal success. If its THOSI status stays very low, even with advantage in natural resources, a society can hardly achieve success because on one hand, the people in such society cannot make full use of such resources due to its broken education system and poor management plus lousy governance, and on the other hand, those THOSI-superior societies (i.e. mainly G7) have the power to absorb such resources through economic or even political and military means. Therefore, we may find lots of examples over the globe to corroborate that natural resources ultimately exert only neutral influence on societal success. These examples are as follows: Japan is a country poor in natural resources except for its beautiful sceneries, but it's still a member to G7, and the same goes for certain European countries; those petro-rich countries in the Middle East and Latin America rely too much on petroleum for its economy and can hardly achieve success; Africa has abundant natural resources, but we can hardly find any successful country there as neck-and-neck with G7; Russia is also rich in natural resources but it has still been struggling with its economy since the collapse of the Soviet Union; Australia, as an ironstone-rich country, can manage its natural resources very well, sell them at fair market value in the world ironstone market and ultimately build its success on the basis of its natural resources together with other factors, and the same goes for the US in terms of its petroleum. Through these specific examples, we can perceive that abundance in natural resources may play a positive role for societal success in those THOSI-superior regions but does not help much with those THOSI-inferior areas and may even in a worse scenario cause nothing but trouble for them (i.e. either relying too much on them to cause economic imbalance and weakness or being dragged into turmoil because of its strategic values in the world economy), which may further reveal the correctness of THOSI Conjecture, i.e. what is ultimately decisive is the THOSI status as well as the consequential human DNA quality or average societal IQ level, rather than abundance in natural resources. In other words, the natural resources on our planet only or mostly serve THOSI-superior regions, instead of the human DNA which is in physical possession of the resources. This is also why the condition in natural resources does not have any seat in THOSI Conjecture. It is simply because it does not have any direct impact on human DNA evolution in the first place.

• So Far So Good of Trumpism from THOSI perspective. Under the THOSI conjecture, it is fair to say that Trumpism has gone so far so good, specifically on the following grounds: 1) building the wall along the US-Mexico border will substantially increase its isolation extent and consequently stabilize and further improve USA's THOSI status (democratic people plus liberals, when speaking of the wall, often compare it with Berlin

Wall and the Great Wall of China, which however were built to mainly prevent slaves from running out of the prison country or resist military aggression by enemies while the US-Mexico wall is solely for the purpose of preventing A-DNA dilution in the US); 2) dispatching illegal / undocumented immigrants will improve DNA quality of its population; 3) cutting off or substantively diminishing visa / immigration programs which are not based on applicant's merit and competitiveness (or DNA quality) but on so-called humanitarian consideration, will also increase the isolation extent, and more importantly absorb quality DNA from other continents (i.e. strengthening the afore-said filtering system) and thus ultimately increase the societal average IQ level, which is the fundamental reason for the US to maintain its super power status over the globe; 4) tax/social welfare cut helps A-DNA Carriers to flourish and at the same time diminishes B-DNA Carriers, and will consequently increase the DNA quality and competitiveness of the whole country; 5) tariff and trade wars, or in other words, fair-trade movement, will offset the disadvantage of the US as brought about by the unbalance between THOSI-superior regions and THOSI-inferior regions, i.e. capital plus talents (quality DNA) and intellectual property (quality social resources) running out of the US and thus dragging down the societal average IQ level and improving other countries in the same regard, and therefore lowering the comparative competitiveness of the US; 6) the proposal to end birthright citizenship through executive order, again, is solely for the purpose of preventing A-DNA dilution in the US; and 7) dragging US forces out of the Middle East will save US a lot of money and energy, and what political systems those messy and war-torn countries in this region should adopt is truly their own matters and the US can hardly help them in this regard since their average societal IQ can as hardly be changed. If we take a more in-depth look into Trumpism for its rationality, we may find that among the five THOSI conditions, the only thing that a federal administration can do about them is to increase the last one, i.e. isolation extent. President Trump perceived that the US isolation extent was quickly declining before his term and that was the root cause for quite many social and economic issues. This answers why Trumpism focuses so much on border and immigration system. Besides, President Trump perceives that a country's success is not exactly based on its political system, culture, history, or natural resources (though very important from business perspective), or whatever as discussed by conventional social science, but is primarily if not solely decided by the DNA quality or societal average IQ level, or in other words, human DNA above all is the most important super-natural resources for a country and thus human DNA quality is quite determinative in terms of its success. So Trumpism also focuses on improvement of DNA quality of US citizens at all cost, which is absolutely right and full of farsightedness. To sum it up, through a long-term observation, we can find that the essence, or the source code, of so-called Trumpism is simply to maintain and strengthen the THOSI superiority of the US and to improve the DNA quality of US citizens in the long run. Under the THOSI Conjecture, Trumpism will indeed make America stronger and more competitive, and undoubtedly will be embraced and applauded by more and more A-DNA Carriers while hated and resisted by more and more B-DNA Carriers. But it should be noted that such ups and downs will not be offset by each other because Trumpism will increase the percentage of A-DNA Carriers along with his presidency, and therefore President Trump is likely to win a bigger victory in the next presidential campaign than he did in his first campaign unless the percentage of B-DNA Carriers in the US is unexpectedly higher than we think, in which case Mr. Trump will probably lose his second campaign to the democrats and more sadly, the B DNA-carriers in the US will flourish again under democratic presidency until such negative trend drags down US economy to such an extent where the majority (no matter they are A-DNA or B-DNA carriers) desperately want a change either in the form of Trumpism or whatever else makes A-DNA carriers flourish. So when hearing those chanted slogans like "America is a country built by immigrants""USA is a country of immigrants", and "we are all immigrants", we may assume that President Trump actually prefers such revised versions as "America is a country mostly built by smart and competitive immigrants" "USA is a country consisting of the quality human genes immigrating from other parts of the world", and "USA only welcomes quality DNA from outside".

• Singapore's unique and fragile success. Singapore is widely seen as a successful country in Asia, especially in terms of its economy, governance, social etiquette, civilization, and hygienic conditions etc. However, it can hardly be seen as a THOSI-superior country, and as a tropical state, its THOSI scores must be much worse than G7. So we need to figure out what are the reasons behind Singapore's success and how to evaluate such success. First of all, the majority of Singaporeans are mainly the descendants of the Chinese who lived along the east coastline in China including Fujian, Guangdong as well as Hainan Island during Ming and Qing Dynasties. These provinces were among the wealthiest places in China at the time, and hence could accommodate and breed quality DNA carriers in China. Due to the difficult living conditions and oppression of the ruling class, certain people chose to leave their home country and start their new life somewhere down in Southeast Asia, i.e. Singapore. These people should have the following personal traits: having upper-level IQ, open-minded, adventurous, courageous, physically and mentally healthy, and hence on an average basis they carried the best of the best DNA in China. Therefore, in that sense the success of Singapore has a very solid genetic basis. Secondly, the Strait of Malacca is extremely advantageous for Singapore in terms of international marine transportation, which flourished after the industrialization revolution in the 18th century. Thirdly, the late Prime Minister of Singapore Mr. Lee Kwan Yew was a leader of unparalleled foresight and sagacity, and most importantly, a

DNA-believer like President Trump. He saw the traits of his fellow Chinese descendants, i.e. diligence, endurance, obedience, selfishness, and a little bit of cowardice (when facing oppressing public power despite their bravery in running away from such power), and accordingly designed the unique political system for Singapore, to fully exploit the potential of his fellow Singaporeans. There are two particular things he did for Singapore worth mentioning, that may confirm the consistency between his mindset and THOSI Conjecture. One is that he decided to install air-conditioners at government buildings on a massive scale to cool down the tropical temperature and get rid of too much humidity (i.e. artificially improving its THOSI status) so that civil servants may work with dignity, quality and efficiency, which well manifested his immense concern or even abhorrence on bad temperature and humidity in tropical area and his ideology that temperature and humidity are critically important for quality human activities, needless to mention human DNA evolution. The other is that Lee decided to enroll senior middle school students and college freshmen, again, on a massive scale from a wide range of reputable high schools and universities in Mainland China from 1990 to 2011 through so-called SM1, SM2 and SM3 scholarship programs based on an international treaty between the central governments of both sides. Under Lee's plan (which is purely designed to absorb quality Chinese DNA), these Chinese students at different school grades entered the high schools and universities in Singapore, graduated from them, found jobs (as a contractual obligation) in Singapore, get married and finally settled in Singapore with citizenship. Only a small portion of these young people finally returned to Mainland China or immigrated to other countries, in particular G7. The whole process seemed so easy, smooth and convenient while the only awkward thing about this massive DNA improvement project is that the Chinese government was so cooperative and supportive when Singapore was so obviously grabbing its quality DNA without paying any price (unless there was certain price according to the above-said treaty and the author's best guess is that Singapore provided training programs for certain batches of Chinese government officials to facilitate China's opening-up policy as determined by the late Chinese leader Deng Xiaoping). Notwithstanding the above, though Singapore is currently a successful tropical country, under the THOSI Conjecture, Singapore's success is unfortunately fragile and unstable due to its inferior THOSI status, and may slip away sooner or later upon satisfaction of most or all of the following conditions: 1) Lee Kwan Yew's successors lack sufficient leadership and authority to maintain the existing governing system; 2) DNA quality in particular average societal IQ level declines as a result of human evolution in THOSI-inferior tropical environment and even air-conditioning can hardly change such downturn; 3) it keeps loosing competitive DNA because of the strong absorption by G7; 4) less competitive DNA keeps pouring in from the neighboring countries in tropical area due to the economic imbalance between Singapore and its neighbors; 4) the Strait Malacca loses its strategic value for any possible reason. Nevertheless, for the time being and in the near future, Singapore will continue to maintain its competitiveness because even a small portion of wealthy people in Mainland China with desire and plan to immigrate to Singapore may function as a quality DNA supply pool for Singapore. Therefore, the above-said slip-away process may take quite a long time from human evolution perspective, be it centuries or even longer.

• China's disputed quick economic development. China's THOSI status in an overall sense is neither bad nor good, but pretty much around or at most a little bit above the mediocre level, so the average human DNA quality in China is unsurprisingly better than most places in Asia, Africa, and Latin America, but definitely lower than G7. And a historical study may reveal that the overall genetic features of Chinese in Mainland China are still not ready for democratic system as originated and flourished in the west. Despite such incompatibility, China, through peaceful and steady development for dozens of years without any massive scale war of aggression from outside world, could repeatedly become one of the top-tier countries in terms of economy, arts, music and literature in a general sense except for science and technology in the ancient dynasties like Han, Tang, Ming, Qing etc. Today, China once again grew to be the second largest economy in the world through unparalleled rapid development for the past few decades under the communist ruling. The logical explanation for such phenomenon is as follows: 1) due to China's mediocre THOSI status, the competitiveness of its average DNA resources stays just at the mid-level as compared with those in G7, and on the other side its A-DNA carriers percentage is very likely to be more or less below the Watershed Percentage and hence the historically never-changing totalitarianism is actually what naturally grows out of such THOSI environment (in their own words, the choice of Chinese people); 2) under such totalitarian political system, people have desire to carry out economic activities to improve their living conditions, and also entertainment-oriented activities to develop the courses of literature, music and arts, etc.; 3) the totalitarian system has the advantage to mobilize and centralize all social and natural resources in the country to focus on big projects, some of which are blessings while some disastrous, much depending on the average IQ level of those on the very top of the ruling class; 4) due to the obedience-oriented values in culture and civilization, people are strongly discouraged to question, doubt, argue and reason, and then logical, creative, innovative and critical thinking is immensely weak in both ancient and present China; 5) because of the above-discussed features, China is always good at producing stuff (i.e. becoming materially prosperous) but lags behind G7 at inventing and originating stuff (i.e. in terms of science and technology) though a very few of Chinese can make remarkable and significant contributions to science and technology due to their more or less connection with G7 (e.g. overseas education and work experience in G7), but on the other hand, China is quite good at inventing those things that do not need much above-said thinking and more importantly pose no threat to the ruling class (e.g. high-tech and fatal weapons), such as tasty food, shining textile, delicate carpentry, nice music, quality literature and arts including beautiful calligraphy etc.; 6) as capped by the average societal IQ level, the combat power or battle effectiveness of China is insufficient for confronting G7, and therefore the country can hardly win any war against the enemies from G7, in particular, Japan, Europe, the US, etc. So on the basis of historical records plus THOSI Conjecture, it can be foreseen that a highly centralized China is very likely to collapse in case of any massive-scale war with the militarily-strong members to G7. However, due to its growing muscles which are at least seemingly powerful and scary, the ruling party's hidden reluctance to get involved in any war with outside power in particular G7 plus G7's own concern on massive-scale refugees and regional economic earthquake, G7 themselves probably are equally reluctant to wage any war against China though G7 may have less tolerance than China does when there has to be a war to sort out their irreconcilable contradictions. Therefore, China is currently in a too-big-to-fail situation and will continue to grow both economically and culturally with its inherent weakness in innovation and creation until its confrontation and contradiction with G7 are irreconcilable, which could be dozens of years or even centuries ahead of us. Therefore, calling for democratic change in China, China taking the place of USA in leading the world, and anticipating or predicting its imminent collapse or a big war between China and outside forces in the near future are either daydreaming or illusionary.

• Categorization of human beings in non-G7 areas from environmental adaptability perspective. Human beings living in non-G7 areas can be roughly categorized into four classes according to their level of ability in adapting themselves to both natural and societal environment. From bottom to top, level four are those who cannot well adapt themselves to the environment and hence are usually not so successful or even regarded as losers struggling with almost everything in their life. Level three are those who can well adapt themselves and hence can make more or less achievements and accomplishments, i.e. living a relatively successful or decent life in non-G7 areas. Level two are those who have the ability to make more achievements or accomplishments than level three but are more demanding for better environment like G7 and fortunately have the excessive ability to flee non-G7 areas and get well settled in G7, i.e. mainly referring to those legal immigrants in G7. So level three are the aforesaid quality DNA pool for G7. And level 1 are the very few who are super-capable of making changes, including changing the environment where they live, i.e. they choose not to flee (although they can) but to stay and make changes according to their own will. If adopting the same four-tier categorization system into G7, the features of level one and level four should be much the same while level two and level three can be merged into one group, i.e. middle and upper (but not top) class. If we take a look at the history over the past few centuries, here is a nonexclusive list of level 1 human beings in both G7 and non-G7 areas: US founding fathers and the most influential presidents like Lincoln, Roosevelt, Regan, and Trump as well as Adolf Hitler, Napoleon Bonaparte, Mao Zedong, Deng Xiaoping, Lee Kwan Yew, Josef Stalin, Vladimir Putin, Boris Yeltsin, Steve Jobs, Bill Gates, Elon Musk, Larry Page, Sergey Brin, Albert Einstein, Isaac Newton, Nikola Tesla, Charles Darwin, Fukuzawa Yukichi and all those who either made miraculous and unparalleled contributions to science and technology plus human society advancement and/or caused massive human disasters.

• Language unification. The number of languages has been shrinking over the past centuries as a result of economic and cultural interaction and competition, and there is no sign or reason that such process will slow down or terminate in the future. On the contrary, it will speed up with development of information technology and artificial intelligence. Along with such process, English as the most widely used language will become increasingly dominant and ultimately be accepted as the unified linguistic system. In other words, more and more population both in G7 and non-G7 areas will give up their own languages and switch to English for varieties of reasons in particular economic consideration. The reason for language unification by English is that the majority of G7, i.e. US, UK, Canada, Australia and New Zealand all adopt English as their official language. Therefore, a large portion of the best minds all over the world are unconsciously nourishing English like a tree day by day and consequently the tree becomes taller and bigger, and in return absorbs more and more quality human DNA functioning as its nutrition. On the other hand, the other languages (even those used in G7 members like Germany, France, Japan and Korea) have to suffer from losing of the said quality human DNA and then will be downgraded to local dialects due to lack of human DNA nutrition and ultimately will fade away. Therefore, the language unification by English as well as its current dominance over the world is not because English was a superior language in the first place but only because it is the best nurtured language and will continue to be so in the future. By nutrition, it may refer to well-translated proverbs and idiomatic expressions in other languages, new concepts coming up along with social, economic, scientific and technological development, sophisticated and ingenious expressions invented or originated by linguistically intelligent people, etc. Fortunately, language unification is a positive thing for the world as it will massively tear down the fundamental differences and barriers between different cultures, and hence will certainly improve mutual understanding and interaction, and solidly built up common values deep in the roots.

- Reform on democratic system. One-man-one-vote suffrage system is the universal democratic system, which however is apparently unreasonable and problematic as the voting right is essentially the right to manage the society and hence it should reflect voter's contribution to the said society, and it should be noted that such arrangement makes more sense not only because it is fairer but also because the said voter's contribution to society usually reflects his IQ and ability to manage the society. Therefore, the voting rules in the corporate world should be partly followed in democratic systems. The most important measurable referential point is certainly the amount of tax paid by individuals while certain other credentials like Nobel Prize or other top prizes, patented inventions, educational background and military service plus ranking etc. can be inter-converted with monetary tax amount. And a person's voting right should be relevant to and proportionate with the specific amount of tax paid by him in certain period of time accordingly. However, one individual's voting right should also be capped no matter how much tax he has paid, so as to prevent the top from politically bullying the rest as well as to protect the rights and interests of lower class at the bottom. Technically speaking, the voting rights can be ranged from 1 to 1,000 (or less). The minimum voting right of one person (even in case of zero tax) is one vote while the wealthiest may have up to 1,000 votes no matter how rich he is. And the rest of voters may fall within the spectrum according to their paid tax amount or other measurable contributions. Through such reformed and improved democratic system, the decisions collectively made by the whole society will be fairer and sounder, and the management of such society will be smarter and more efficient, while the human rights of the lower class at bottom can also be reasonably respected and protected. One-man-one-vote ideology derived from "all men are created equal" cliché, which is simply wrong because it is repeatedly proved to be the very truth that men are unequally created genetically either by chance or by inheritance, although they should be given equal opportunities to figure out who are genetically superior or inferior or mediocre and hence should proportionately enjoy their voting rights. Such system works very well and smoothly in the corporate world and there is simply no reason why it would fail in the political arena.

• Global governance reform under THOSI Conjecture. As implied by THOSI Conjecture, it is unavoidable to take the following steps to fundamentally change the current chaotic, messy, disorganized and inefficient global governance via the United Nations system and hopefully to achieve real peace and stability as well as sustainable development on the earth. Step one is the union of G7 which should ultimately be merged into one state that is governed under only one military, political, economic and social system, so that all citizens, capital, goods and services in G7 can freely move or trade within G7. More importantly, the said union and merger of G7 will also create a military super power (more powerful and more united than NATO) that is globally dominant and cannot be challenged by any or all of non-G7 regimes. Step two is the conquer of non-G7 areas through negotiations, coercions and even military interference, aiming at surrender of the ruling parties of non-G7 areas and dismantling / eradicating / eliminating their military organizations while maintaining their ruling status (mainly through police power) as the consideration (price) for their cooperation and surrender. Obviously step two is a long hard process full of bitterness which may take decades or even centuries, and this is why it must come after step one which can centralize all of the resources within G7 and thus make the united G7 politically dominant and militarily invincible. Otherwise step two would be either infeasible or dangerous and devastating. Step three is to restructure the surrendered non-G7 areas into five big zones, i.e. zone one for Africa, zone two for Asia, zone three for Latin America, zone four for the Middle East, and zone five for Oceanic. During step three, another important task is to implement tailored colonization system as adopted by Britain during the 17th-19th centuries in these five zones one by one instead of concurrently. It is noteworthy that the current democratic system in G7 cannot be applied into the five zones as such system is incompatible with their human DNA status. Step four is well-regulated and free-competition-based channeling of quality human DNA (i.e. A-DNA carriers) from these five zones to G7, and shrinkage of population of B-DNA carriers in the five zones in a civilized, humanitarian and peaceful way (e.g. one-child policy) until the remaining population in each of the five zones is small enough to be absorbed or digested by G7. In other words, the boundaries segregating G7 and the five zones can be finally removed without posing any threat to the human DNA quality of G7, i.e. maintaining the Watershed Percentage. Step five is to divide the five zones into two sections, with section one having similar latitude as G7, i.e. with human-friendly temperature, humidity, oxygen concentration and sunlight intensity (e.g. South Africa, certain countries in South America, some areas in China, etc.), and section two covering the rest (i.e. with inferior-THOSI status), which is then followed by the evacuation of human DNA from section two to section one or G7, and then utilizing artificial intelligence and robots in these mandatorily unpopulated zones for energy and food production so the natural resources in such areas are not wasted. For the purpose of equal and sound human DNA evolution, human residence within section two should be strictly restricted or even prohibited after the evacuation, as a positive result of which, the ecological environment in section two can also be restored.

• White attractiveness and privilege. A sensitive but popular question is whether beauty of certain ethnic groups in particular white Caucasians is primarily based on social influence. The answer should be no and here is why: 1) Every piece or portion of human appearance (color of skin, hair, eye, teeth, shape of eye, ear, nose, mouth, face, skull, shoulder, breast, butt, waist, legs, etc. as well as the proportion and composition between one another) can be analyzed from aesthetic perspective and we can surely spot the perfection point on a spectrum through empirical study. 2) Taking skin color as an example: if the color of a person (either Caucasian or with other ethnicity) is as pale as white paper, it certainly freaks people out or at least makes you feel uncomfortable, but if it's darker than average Asian skin color, it's also visually far from perfection. So the perfection point could be somewhere between brown and pure white. This is very much like Word file background color. If we are only allowed to choose a color between extreme white and extreme black, the perfection point should be kind of grey because it makes our eyes feel most comfortable. 3) Of course different people may have slightly different perfection points (i.e. more or less grey), but here we are discussing the issue on an average basis. In other words, generally speaking, most people tend to have their Word file background at certain level of grey. And the same goes for human being's skin color. So the essence of this issue can really be translated down to what kind of skin color makes human eyes most comfortable. If it's too dark, your eyes will more easily get tired especially at a place where light is not so strong, but if it's too white, your eyes certainly will get uncomfortable in another way around. 4) So it is quite understandable why so many people around the world are so obsessed with the skin color of white Caucasians. They are actually not influenced by media or culture or education, i.e. it is not a social construct. They are just being honest to themselves, specifically speaking, to their very eyes. But from individual perspective, race (or skin color or appearance) really does not matter so much, because what mainly determines a person's competitiveness and future is his or her IQ. So everyone, as long as he or she is smart enough, will certainly achieve success if they try hard enough.

• THOSI and racism. THOSI Conjecture is based on observation and reasoning, hence it has nothing to do with racism although it may arouse discussion on whether THOSI is in itself racist or leads to racism. Furthermore, there is fundamental difference between the two. Racism has so far not been precisely defined but the pivotal part of racism is the discrimination against certain ethnic group only on the basis of their ethnicity without looking into every individual's merits and characters. Speaking of discrimination, it must refer to certain specific unjust or prejudicial treatment. Therefore, the constitution of racism or racist practice must be subject to, among others, these two indispensable elements: 1) judging a person wholly or mainly according to his ethnicity; and 2) that person is treated with inferior conditions as compared with other ethnic groups. But if we take a look at THOSI Conjecture, element one does not exist at all because under THOSI Conjecture if a person in non-G7 areas can legally immigrate into G7 (i.e. on a fair-competition basis), no matter what ethnic group he belongs to or comes from, the human DNA carried by this person shall be regarded as the same with or even more competitive than the average human DNA in G7. In addition, under THOSI Conjecture, all human beings should be legally, socially, and economically treated in an equal manner while politically should be treated on a pro-rata basis (i.e. in accordance with their paid tax amounts or other measurable contributions) rather than on a racial basis. Thus element two does not exist in the THOSI Conjecture either. Notwithstanding the above, the reason that THOSI Conjecture may arouse racist concern is that people have been long prohibited or discouraged to openly discuss the differences between different people in different geographical areas, which are mistakenly associated with the differences between different races or ethnic groups and hence become unreasonably sensitive and then little by little grow to be an enemy of political-correctness that may endanger or jeopardize the career life of scholars, politicians, businesspersons etc. almost in all walks of life. Therefore, talking about genetic differences between different ethnic groups in the west becomes as dangerous as talking about whether communism is a good idea in communist countries in the east. Last but not the least, THOSI Conjecture not only rejects racism but also helps address the issues incurred by racism because it helps us courageously face up to the very differences between different geographical areas plus the underlying reasons, and ultimately understand that those human beings migrating to, settling and evolving in those THOSI-superior areas are simply more lucky in a geographical and genetic sense but are not and never will be superior than the other human beings in terms of humanity and dignity. In short, men are not created equal, but should be treated equally.